Richard Richardson

The genealogy of the Richardson family of the state of Delaware

Richard Richardson

The genealogy of the Richardson family of the state of Delaware

ISBN/EAN: 9783337732066

Printed in Europe, USA, Canada, Australia, Japan

Cover: Foto ©ninafisch / pixelio.de

More available books at **www.hansebooks.com**

Richard Richardson

The genealogy of the Richardson family of the state of Delaware

ISBN/EAN: 9783337732066

Printed in Europe, USA, Canada, Australia, Japan

Cover: Foto ©ninafisch / pixelio.de

More available books at **www.hansebooks.com**

THE

GENEALOGY

OF THE

RICHARDSON FAMILY

OF THE

STATE OF DELAWARE.

BY

RICHARD RICHARDSON.

PRINTED FOR PRIVATE DISTRIBUTION.
1878.

The design of this publication is principally intended to preserve the history of the earlier generations of the Richardson family in this country. We are unable to trace their origin any further back, nothing being known of their English pedigree. The knowledge of the history of some of the branches, in the second and third generations, is already lost, and what is known of the others is possessed by but a few, and is also likely to pass into oblivion if not kept alive in print.

This account is carried down to the beginning of the eighth generation in this country, commencing with John Richardson, the first emigrant, which is as far as it has reached at present. It does not profess to be complete in all the details, but the foundation has been laid upon which others may build, enlarge, and perfect the structure. It is printed in such form that dates may be filled in with the pen, which every family can do for themselves.

It will be apparent to the reader that the family has not been a prolific one, compared with many others; and that the name is in imminent danger of running out; there being at present not one male descendant in the seventh, and but four in the sixth generation, that bear the name of Richardson.

This work is intended for the use of the family alone, to whom it is hoped it may prove interesting and valuable ; from several of whom, important information in relation to it has been obtained.

The dates given, when previous to 1752, are old, after that date they are new style.

R. R.

PHILADELPHIA, 1878.

SYNOPSIS OF NAMES AND DATES.

FIRST GENERATION.

Names.	Birth.	Death.	Married.	Date.	Index.
John Richardson . . .		1710	Elizabeth —— . . .		9

SECOND GENERATION.

Richard Richardson . .					15
—— Richardson . . .			James Anderson . . .		15
John Richardson . . .	1679	1755	Ann Ashton	1704	15

THIRD GENERATION.

Elizabeth Richardson . .	1705	1734	Unmarried		28
Joseph Richardson . . .	1706	1770	Sarah Morris	1744	28
Robert Richardson . . .	1708	1761	Sarah Shipley	1750	29
Susanna Richardson . .	1710	1766	Peter Bayard		30
Sarah Richardson . . .	1712	1772	Dr. John Finney . . .	1742	31
Ann Richardson	1714	1799	William Armstrong . .	1758	31
Mary Richardson . . .	1715	1798	Peter Reeve	1772	32
Rebecca Richardson . .	1717	1773	Joseph Peters	1741	33
			William Morris . . .	1752	33
John Richardson . . .	1718	1737	Unmarried		34
Richard Richardson .	1720	1797	Sarah Tatnall	1766	34
Hannah Richardson .	1721	1787	Thomas Gray	1752	37
			Francis Johnson . . .		37
Jane Richardson . . .	1727	1805	Dr. John McKinly . .		38

FOURTH GENERATION.

Sarah Richardson . . .	1746	1825	Nicholas Waln . . .	1771	40
Elizabeth Richardson . .	1751	1782	Charles Wilcox . . .	1778	40
John Richardson . . .	1753	1800	Unmarried		41
Mary Richardson . . .	1758	1795	Unmarried		41

(v)

Names.	Birth.	Death.	Married.	Date.	Index.
Ann Richardson . . .	1760	1838	Dr. Henry Latimer . .	1789	41
Ann Bayard			—— Scott		42
John R. Bayard . . .	1739	1756	Unmarried		42
Susanna Bayard . . .			Jonathan Smith . . .		42
Elizabeth Bayard . . .			—— Rogers	1752	42
Joseph Richardson . . .	1767	1833	Ann Spackman . . .	1803	43
John Richardson . . .	1769	1773	Unmarried		43
Elizabeth Richardson . .	1771	1847	Samuel Stroud . . .	1789	43
Richard Richardson . .	1774	1774			44
Ashton Richardson . .	1776	1852	Mary Wood	1807	44
Ann Richardson . .	1778	1845	Unmarried		45
John Richardson . . .	1783	1859	Margaret Paxson . . .	1813	45

FIFTH GENERATION.

Joseph Waln	1770	1782	Unmarried		46
William Waln . . .	1775	1825	Mary Wilcox	1805	46
Nicholas Waln . .	1778	1849	Unmarried		46
Mary Waln			Died in infancy . . .		46
Jacob S. Waln . .	1783	1847	Unmarried		46
Sarah Latimer			1828	Unmarried		46
John R. Latimer . . .	1793	1865	Elizabeth Kepley . . .	1834	46
Mary R. Latimer . . .	1796	1871	Unmarried		46
Henry Latimer . . .	1799		Sarah Ann Baily . . .	1822	46
James Latimer	1802	1837	Unmarried		46
Martha Scott					46
John R. Smith					46
Mary Smith . . .					46
Samuel Smith					46
Susanna Smith					46
John R. Rogers					47
Susanna Rogers			Wm. Tennant		47
Jane Richardson . . .	1805	1839	Samuel S. Poole . . .	1837	47
Samuel S. Richardson . .	1806		Susan Robinson . . .	1841	47
Sarah Richardson . . .	1808	1839	Unmarried		47
Thomazin Richardson .	1810				47
Edward T. Richardson .	1812	1877	Hannah Masden . . .	1841	47
Joseph Richardson . . .	1814				47

Names.	Birth.	Death.	Married.	Date.	Index.
George Richardson . .	1816		Sarah Woolston . . .	1845	47
Ann Stroud	1795		Stephen Pancoast . .	1820	47
Mary Stroud	1797	1821	Stephen Bonsall . . .	1819	47
Edward Stroud	1800	1821	Unmarried		47
Samuel Stroud	1803	1866	Mary E Jones	1829	47
Sarah R. Stroud	1806	1875	Jesse Mendinhall . . .	1830	48
James Stroud	1811		Hannah F. Hedges . .	1835	48
Richard Richardson . .	1808		Hannah White . . .	1841	48
Robert W. Richardson .	1810	1869	Elizabeth R. Hulme . .	1847	48
Elizabeth Richardson . .	1812	1867	William Hodgson . .	1835	48
Mary Richardson . . .	1815		Thomas Wistar . . .	1867	48
Sarah Richardson . . .	1817	1876	Joseph Tatnall . . .	1841	48
Hannah W. Richardson .	1819				48
Lucy Richardson . . .	1824		John R. Tatum . . .	1852	48
Ashton Richardson . .	1830				48
Sarah T. Richardson . .	1815	1861	Edward T. Bellach . .	1856	48
Anna Richardson . . .	1816		Joseph Bringhurst . .	1842	49
William P. Richardson .	1818		Mary W. Forst . . .	1865	49
Elizabeth Richardson . .	1819		Joseph C. Turnpenny .	1853	49
Mary Richardson . . .	1821		Charles Warner . . .	1843	49
John Richardson . . .	1824		Martha Andrews . . .	1856	49
Joseph P. Richardson . .	1825		Sarah Andrews . . .	1856	49

SIXTH GENERATION.

John Waln			Died unmarried . .	50
Sarah Waln . .			Benjamin C. Wilcox	50
Nicholas Waln				50
William Waln				50
Mary Waln			Dr. — Maxwell . .	50
Elizabeth Latimer . . .				50
Henry Latimer . .				50
Anna Latimer . .				50
Joseph B. Latimer . . .		1860	Unmarried	50
John Latimer				50
Mary Latimer				50
Ann S. Richardson .		1843	John Sellers Bancroft .	1871	50
Elizabeth R. Richardson .	1845	1869	Jno. Sellers Bancroft .	1866	50

SEVENTH GENERATION.

EIGHTH GENERATION.

GENEALOGY

RICHARDSON FAMILY.

FIRST GENERATION.

THE earliest ancestor of our family, of whom we have any account, emigrated to this country in or about the year 1682. This was John Richardson (whom I shall designate as the first). He came from a town in Lincolnshire, England, called at that time Glamford Bridge (now "Brigg"), a market town in the northern part of that county.

Proud, in his History of Pennsylvania, page 218, in a note, says: "Of the Quakers that settled in and about New Castle in the year 1682, were John Hussy, JOHN RICHARDSON, Edw. Blake, &c."

"John Hussy, JOHN RICHARDSON, Edw. Blake, Benj. Swett, and other Friends, being settled in and near New Castle, held a meeting for worship several years at private houses in said town; it was first set up by the authority of the yearly meeting of Phila. the 2d of the first month 1684, and continued until 1705, when a lot of ground was purchased, and a

2

meeting house was built, which has since been enlarged as it is at present."*

As regards the time of his emigration to this country, we have no precise knowledge. In the "Register of Arrivals in Philadelphia," in the Library of the Historical Society of Pennsylvania, at Philadelphia, it is stated that a "John Richardson arrived at Philadelphia in the Ship Endeavour, Capt. Geo. Thorp, the 20th of the 7th mo. 1683." This may have been our ancestor; but as there was more than one John Richardson that came from England, we cannot be certain that this was he. There has been a tradition in the family, which I have heard from my father and grandmother, that he emigrated in the same ship that brought over Robert Ashton; if that be the case, the date may be fixed as being the 8th of the third month, 1686. But this is several years later than the other dates. The two accounts may be reconciled, if we conclude that John Richardson came in advance of his family, and that they came with Robert Ashton, which is not improbable. So the matter will have to be left in uncertainty. His wife's name was Elizabeth ———, but this is all that is known respecting her. His children were, as appears from his will, two sons, John and Richard, and a daughter, whose name is not mentioned, married to a James Anderson, of George's Creek, Delaware.

He left nearly the whole of his estate (not pre-

---

* See Smith's History of Pennsylvania, published in Hazard's Register.

viously given to them), to his two sons, after the death of his widow, without specifying what it was, or where situated; it is therefore impossible to give any information about it. He had real estate at New Castle. He was a member of the Assembly for New Castle County in the year 1697, as appears from the minutes of the Council held the "12th of May, 1697," at Philadelphia. (*See* Colonial Records.) He also held the office of Justice of the Peace (a more important office than now) under Wm. Penn's government, as appears from a notice published in the Franklin Journal, Vol. IV., No. 1, page 11, 1842, describing the mode of the laying out the curve of the northern boundary of the State of Delaware in 1701, viz :

Extract from Wm. Penn's order for making said survey :

" 1st. The original warrant of Wm. Penn as Proprietor and Governor of the Province of Penna. and Counties annexed, bearing date the 28th of the 8th mo., 1701, directed to Isaac Taylor, of the County of Chester, in the Province of Penna., and Thos. Pierson, of the County of New Castle in the territories, instructing them to accompany the magistrates of each County, or any three of them, &c."

Extract from the surveyor's memoranda :

" The 26th day of the 9th mo. we did begin, in the presence of the said Justices, Rich. Hallowell, JOHN RICHARDSON, Caleb Pusey, Philip Roman, and Robert Pyle, Esq's, at the end of the horse dyke in the town of N. Castle, &c. &c."

I also find in the minutes of the Provincial Council his name appended to a certificate laid before the Council by a certain Thos. Woolston, complaining of another person not obeying a decree of the provincial judges; this came before the Council 7th mo. 2, 1688. The magistrates at that time constituted the Provincial Courts of Justice. There are several other Richardsons mentioned in "Proud's History of Pennsylvania" and other places: another John Richardson, who must not be confounded with our ancestor, who was a member of Wm. Penn's first Council, and died in 1700; also, Samuel Richardson, a member of Council, and many times Prothonotary of Philadelphia, &c. &c., from whom the Richardsons of Bucks County, Pennsylvania, have descended, and Wm. Richardson, Choptank, Maryland, David Richardson, &c., but it is not known that they are relatives of ours.

John Richardson's death occurred on the 19th of the 11th mo. 1710, and his remains were probably interred in the Friends' burial ground at New Castle, where the family still have a private lot walled in; as the date of his birth is not known, it is not possible to state his age. It is not known how long his wife survived him. He had a brother Joseph Richardson in England, to whose son John he left a small legacy.

His will is dated the "11th of November," and he died the 19th of the same month. The will is as follows:—

In the name of God, amen. I, John Richardson, of New Castle, in the County of New Castle, on Delaware, being sick and weak in body, but of sound and perfect mind and memory, thanks be to Almighty God for the same, do make this my last will and testament in manner and form following, that is to say,

First, and principally, I commit my soul into the hands of Almighty God, hoping through the merits and death and passion of my Saviour

Jesus Christ, to have full and free pardon and forgiveness of all my sins, and to inherit everlasting life. And my body I commit to the earth to be decently buried, at the discretion of my executors hereafter named. And, as touching the disposition of such temporal estate as it has pleased Almighty God to bestow upon me, I give and dispose of as follows, viz.:

First, I will that all such debts as I owe in right to any person whatsoever, together with my funeral charges and probate of this my last will, be paid and discharged.

Item. I give and bequeath unto my dear and loving wife Elizabeth, all my money, plate, cattle, household goods, chattels, and debts due me, and all and singular my personal estate, whatsoever and wheresoever, to her own proper use, by her to be disposed of as she shall have occasion for, towards her maintenance and comfortable subsistence and living, during the term of her natural life; and, further, that my said loving wife shall hold possession and enjoy all such real estate as I shall die possessed of, for and during the term of her natural life, and shall take the rents and profits thereof to her own proper use.

Item. This is my will and mind, and I do hereby desire my two sons, John and Richard, to pay unto my said wife yearly, and every year, for the term of her natural life, (if her necessities require and demand the same,) all such sums of money and effects as I have reserved to myself out of the profits of the estate I have heretofore given them.

Item. I give unto my grandson, James Anderson, son of James Anderson, of St. George's, yeoman, the sum of Ten Pounds, old currency.

Item. I give unto my granddaughter, Mary Anderson, daughter of said James Anderson, Twenty Pounds, old currency.

Item. I give unto my nephew, John Richardson, son of my brother Joseph Richardson, of Glamford Bridge, in the County of Lincoln, in the Kingdom of Great Britain, woolen draper, the sum of Ten Pounds, old currency. The said sums of money by me given as aforesaid to my two grandchildren and my nephew, shall be paid to them respectively within the space of twelve months next after the decease of my said wife Elizabeth, out of such personal estate as she my said wife shall die possessed of, after her funeral charges are paid and discharged; and it is my will and mind that in case the personal estate whereof my said wife shall die possessed of after her funeral expenses are discharged, shall not amount to so much as will pay the aforesaid legacies, then all or so much of my real estate as aforesaid as shall be thought necessary, shall be sold and disposed of for the payment of the same, and that in case either of my grandchildren or nephew shall happen to depart this life before the expiration of one whole year next after the decease of my said wife, or the payment of their respective legacies, which of them shall first happen, then it is my will and mind that the part or share of such person so dying as aforesaid shall be paid to my two sons, John and Richard Richardson, equally to be divided between them or to their heirs, in case of the death of either of them.

Item. I give and bequeath to my two sons John and Richard, and their heirs forever, all and every such estate real and personal whatsoever and wheresoever, as shall be left by my said wife undisposed of at the time of her death, after her debts are paid and her funeral expenses discharged, together with the aforesaid legacies, equally divided between them, and in case of the death of either of my two sons, before such division of the remainder of said estate, then the share of him dying aforesaid shall be equally distributed among his children.

And, lastly, I do hereby make and appoint my dear and loving wife Elizabeth, and my said son John Richardson executors of this my last will and testament, and I do hereby revoke and make void all other wills and testaments whatsoever by me at any time heretofore made either in word or writing.

In witness whereof, I, the said testator, have hereunto set my hand and seal the 10th day of November, in the ninth year of the reign of Queen Anne, of Great Britain, 1710.

JOHN RICHARDSON. [SEAL.]

Signed, sealed, published and declared by the said testator as his last will and testament in the presence of us,

    GEORGE HOGG, Sen.,

    BEVING T. SWALT.

    WILLIAM GEORGE.

Copy from the original on record in the office of the Register of Wills at New Castle, Book B, page 224.

SECOND GENERATION.

RICHARD RICHARDSON, son of John and Elizabeth Richardson. Of this person nothing is known except what is mentioned in the will of his father. It is uncertain whether he ever was in this country, though his father's will would seem to indicate it. It is pretty certain, however, that he left no descendants in this country.

———— RICHARDSON, daughter of John and Elizabeth. She is mentioned in John Richardson's will as having married "James Anderson of St. Georges, Yeoman," to whose two children, Mary and James, he left a Legacy of Ten Pounds each. This is all the information there is respecting this branch of the family.

JOHN RICHARDSON the second, son of John and Elizabeth, was born in England in 1679, and emigrated to this country with his parents when a child, in the year 1682 or thereabouts. He married Ann Ashton daughter of Robert and Elizabeth Ashton, of St. Georges, New Castle Co., Delaware, at a Friends meeting, held at her father's house the 7th of the 7th month, 1704; as appears from the marriage certificate extant: he being 25 years of age, and she a year

younger or thereabouts. He settled on the banks of
the Christiana Creek about two miles above the present City of Wilmington, on the first point of upland
on the north side of said creek above Wilmington,
and owned nearly all the land bordering on the creek
as high up and including the "Folly woods" as it is
now called. It was his intention to found a town
there, the plan being arranged and the streets laid out
on paper; but in this he was disappointed, the site of
Wilmington being nearer the river Delaware, super-
seded it. He and his sons carried on a considerable
mercantile trade from this place, having wharves and
storehouses there, transporting sugar and molasses and
other West Indian products in vessels of their own;
his sons going out with the vessels as commanders and
supercargoes, and for that day did a large business;
in which he was prosperous and amassed a considerable estate, both real and personal. His old mansion
house, with an addition built in 1743, was standing
until the year 1833, when it was taken down, the
walls being cracked and in a weak condition. The
present house is on the same site, and the old bricks
were used in the construction of the new house. The
old one was quite a curiosity in its way; having
leaden sashes in the windows, etc. etc. An old corner cupboard, a relic of the furniture of John Richardson, is still preserved in the house. It belongs to
Henry Latimer, a descendant of Robert Richardson. The house and land were left by will to John
Richardson, son of Robert Richardson, (by his grand-

father, John Richardson,) who dying childless and intestate, it descended to his sister, Ann Latimer, as heir-at-law.

John Richardson was a member of the Assembly for the three lower counties, now the State of Delaware, for the year 1716 and frequently afterwards; he also held the office of Justice of the Peace and Judge of the Provincial Court, was a man held in general esteem, and of unblemished character.

It is mentioned in "Smith's History of Pennsylvania" (see Hazard's Register) that "a monthly meeting of Friends was held in a private house the 2d of 3 mo. 1686, and was composed of Friends living in the said town, and near Christiana and White Clay Creeks and the east side of the Brandywine, and continued to be held at N. Castle till the 1st month, 1687, when it was moved to Newark, and held at Valentine Hollingsworth, Cornelius Empson, and Morgan Derwitt's for the ease of the members thereof, until the year 1704, at which time it was moved to the centre, and held by turns at N. Castle, Newark and Centre, and sometimes at the house of JOHN RICHARDSON; this continued until 1715."

The following is a copy of the marriage certificate of John Richardson and Ann Ashton, in my possession :—

Whereas, John Richardson Jr. of the County of New Castle and near Christeen Creek ; and Ann Ashton of George's Creek of said County, having declared their intention of marriage with each other in our monthly meeting of the people called Quakers, belonging to

3

Newark, whose proceedings therein, after enquiry made of both parties and consent of friends and relations concerned, they being free from all others, were approved of by the said meeting &c.—Now these are to certify all whom it may concern that for the full accomplishment of their said intentions this 7th day of the Seventh month in the year 1704, the said John Richardson Jr. and Ann Ashton did appear in a public meeting appointed for that service, of the said people at the house of Robert Ashton in the abovesaid County, when the said John Richardson Jr. taking the said Ann Ashton by the hand, did solemnly declare as follows—viz—" Friends in the presence of God and this assembly, I take this my friend Ann Ashton to wife, promising by the Lord's assistance to be unto her a true and faithful husband until it may please God by death to separate us:" and then and there in the said assembly the said Ann Ashton did declare as follows—viz. "friends in the presence of God and this assembly, I take this my friend John Richardson Jr. to be my husband, promising with God's assistance to be a faithful and loving wife until it please God by death to separate us."—In confirmation thereof the said John Richardson and Ann Ashton did then and there to these presents subscribe their names as husband and wife—and we whose names are underwritten being present at the solemnization of said marriage as witnesses thereto, having sett to our hands the day and year above written.

JOHN RICHARDSON
ANN RICHARDSON.

John Richardson*	John French	James Crawford
Robert Ashton*	Ebenezer Empson	Mary Smith
Sarah Wyate†	Antho: Morris	Hannah Parkin
Jno. Ashton†	Geo. Harlin	Ann Thompson
Joseph Ashton†	Thos. Hollingsworth	Rebecca Reed
Thomas Chalkley	Michl. Harlin	Sarah Hogg
R. D. Haes	William Thompson	Sarah Griffin
Hercules Coots	Jno. Empson	Sarah Parkin

Recorded page 73, in the Monthly Meeting Book, by

JOSEPH MENDINGALL, Clerk.

* The parents of the parties married.
† Sister and brothers of the bride.

He died the 4th of the 9th mo. 1755, aged 76 years, and was interred at New Castle in the family burial lot, it is believed.

His children were Elizabeth, Joseph, Robert, Susanna, Sarah, Ann, Mary, Rebecca, John, Richard, Hannah, and Jane Richardson.

His will is dated "the 20th day of the 12th mo. called December 1752," with codicil, dated "the 6th day of August 1755," and is as follows, viz:—

Copy of John Richardson's Will.

In the name of God, amen; this the twentieth day of the twelfth month called December in the year of our Lord one thousand seven hundred and fifty-two, Anno Domini &c. 1752. I, John Richardson, of the County of New Castle and Christiana Hundred on Delaware, being in perfect health and strength of body and perfect mind and memory, but calling to mind the uncertainty of this life on earth, do make this my last will and testament in manner and form following, hereby revoking and making null and void all other will or wills, testament or testaments heretofore made by me, either in word or writing, and this to be taken for my last will and no other.—

First. That all such debts and duties, as I owe in right to any person or persons whatsoever, together with my funeral charges and probate of my will, be well and truly paid by my executors hereafter named, within convenient time after my decease. And as to such worldly estate as it has pleased God in his bounty to bestow upon me, I give and devise and dispose of as followeth—viz:—Item, I give and grant unto my three daughters which are unmarried Ann, Mary, and Jane, full privilege of my new dwelling house which I now live in meaning that part built about nine years ago, and the cellar which is under it, as also the privilege in the orchard for apples, and garden for house use, and privilege for wood for firewood off from their brother Roberts land, which I hereafter give to him, during their keeping unmarried. But when any of them shall marry then shall be barred and lose that privilege. But if there be two of them which may be unmarried they shall keep it, and if but one, she shall still keep the privilege of two rooms in the dwelling house and cellar.

Item. I give and devise unto my son Joseph Richardson my houses and lots of land in the town of New Castle, both them which the weaver lately dwelt in, as also that on the river side where the old store and stable stands on, which I bought of Joseph Wood and Ebenezer Empson, with all the houses and other lots which in any way belongeth to me in the town of New Castle, to him the said Joseph Richardson his heirs and assigns forever.

Item. I give and devise unto my son Robert Richardson, all that land and building, wharf and storehouse where Edward Carter at present dwells, called Safe Harbour, meaning all that said tract, and that called Powell Point, all containing about 300 acres be it more or less, excepting what is hereafter reserved for my son Richard, and privilege for wood for my daughters. And also I give and devise to him my present dwelling house and land, being about 35 acres, as also three pieces of marsh or medow ground, one piece containing about 13 acres which I bought of Peter Poulson, what lays right over Christiana Creek, against the aforesaid wharf, as also 15 acres of the marsh below Double Sprout which lays on the said Sprout and Christiana Creek, as also the marsh called the Drain Marsh by the orchard and home place; to him and his heirs and assigns forever, excepting what is hereafter reserved for his brother Richard, as also the privileges to his sisters as aforementioned.

Item. I give and devise to my son Richard Richardson ten acres of land off from his brother Robert's land joining on George Robertson's land, which he bought of Jasper Walraven, from Christiana Creek to the Kings Road leading to Newport, meaning parallel from the creek to the road along the said Robinson's line; with privilege for fire wood from his brother Roberts land for two fires if Robert or his heirs shall live thereon, to him his heirs and assigns forever, meaning the ten acres, but if he doth sell or dispose of the said 10 acres the privilege of firewood shall cease and remain in his brother Robert's property. I do also further give and devise to my son Rich'd Richardson all that tract of land called Content or Swamp, as also that plantation whereon Richard Groves dwells with the house and all improvements thereon : as also the mill lands, and mill and the house and improvements which is thereupon or in anywise belonging to the same, and all the marsh which layeth all along down Mill Creek and joyning to James Sinex's and Gisbert Walraven's marsh to him and his heirs and assigns forever. Also further it is my will that if either of my sons Robert or Richard should die and leave no lawful heirs, nor dispose of the same by either of them who had a right to such share or part, and the other of them shall have at that time any child or children, then that share or part so bequested, meaning the land and marsh shall go to the survivor of them and their heirs or assigns. But if no lawful heirs, then to be shared equally amongst the brothers and sisters living, or their lawful issue if such be.—And further if both my sons Robert and Richard should die and leave no lawful heirs, nor the lands sold by them in their lifetime, then to be equally divided among the surviving children, or if any of them should be deceased and leave child or children, shall have that share or part which their parents had right to if alive. And inasmuch as I conceive Robert's share of the real estate rather exceeds his brother Richards, I therefore give and bequeath to my son Rich Richardson on a certain mortgage which I have on Gisbert Walravens plantation before any division of my personal estate be shared &c.— Now inasmuch as my real estate is shared and bequested amongst my three sons and to them their heirs and assigns forever. And inasmuch as the chief part of my estate is in outstanding debts as Mortgages, Bonds, Bills &c. I do hereby authorise and empower my executors hereinafter named to pass deed of conveyance to John Hannum for the half of the mill and lands at Doe Run, who has passed or given bond for the same as may appear by the agreement with him under hand and seal to convey my right to him, he complying with his part. My further will is that my executors pay in one years time after my death, Ten Pistoles, apiece to my seven grandchildren namely Ann Bayard, John Bayard, Susanna Bayard, children of Peter and my daughter Susanna Bayard, and to Sarah Richardson daughter of my son Joseph, and to Elizabeth Richardson, daughter of my son Robert, and to John Finney and Sarah Finney children of Dr. Finney and Sarah his wife, which makes Seventy Pistoles amongst them all seven.—My further will is that my daughter Sarah Finney who is married to Dr. Finney to have Five Hundred Pounds to be made up with what she has received, which is charged in Book A, and Two Hundred Pounds more lawful money of this government if she live to be a widow, or otherwise to her child or children if she have any three years after my death, and not before then to be paid by my executors, either to her if a widow, or to her child or children which is to be her full share and no more. And my daughter Rebecca Morris wife to Wm. Morris having a considerable estate and no child shall have One hundred pounds more than she already has had which is charged in my book A, to be paid her one year after my death by my executors which shall be her full share of my estate.

And as my daughter Hannah who has lately married Thomas Gray, contrary to my desire or consent and for her disobedience she shall have but Two Hundred Pounds, to be paid her two years after my decease and not before, or to her child if she should have any at the time, (if she should be dead), paid by my executors, and she is hereby utterly barred from any more of my estate whatsoever.—My further will is that all the rest of my estate of what nature or kind soever it is of, excepting the land, already divided aforesaid, be equally shared amongst all the rest of my children namely (after legacies paid as aforesaid) Joseph, Robert, Richard, Ann, Mary, and Jane Richardson, but if any of my three daughters namely, Ann, Mary or Jane should marry, without the consent of their brothers or friends then should have but Five Hundred pounds, for their full share of my estate. And as I have given all my children something some more and some less and it is all charged in book called A, which I keep for that purpose and charged with my own hand for which sums they are to deduct such out of their portions or shares &c. It is my further will if any of my daughters should be so reduced that they want the necessaries of life then my two sons Robert and Richard shall supply their wants as they have the largest portion.—It is my further will that all my household goods, Horses, Cattle and Sheep and plantation utensils and all other goods of what nature or kind soever they may be of, as part of two Brigantines the Sally and Fox, and the sloop Lark, be put into one inventory, and after the above portions and legacies are paid as aforesaid, all the remainder of the movables be equally divided among my six children aforesaid, Joseph, Robert, Richard, Ann, Mary, and Jane, (if none marry contrary to consent aforesaid), and cast up, which my will is that they be equally divided between my six children aforesaid, only as before observed my children which have received some part which is charged in a book before mentioned which I have given them be first deducted out of their dividends, that my movables may be as equally divided amongst the six as it can be, if they marry by consent as afore observed. And if any dispute arise either amongst my children or any other person or persons whatsoever, in any condition, whatever it may be, to agree, make up, discharge and settle by composition arbitration or otherwise, and if any difference about any thing wherein I am or at the time of my death should be intrusted or concerned, I do hereby empower my executors so to do. And lastly my will is that my executors shall have Fifty Pounds for their commissions and no more, by reason that the chief trouble will be to inventory the whole estate and make a division. The land is shared by will, all but such as is sold, which must be conveyed as aforesaid &c. And inasmuch as there are few or no debts to pay, my will is that what share that falls to my daughters may be in large sums out of bonds and mortgages, and the smaller debts, and such as seem to be most doubtful to be safe, for that reason with all speed they seek to secure such debts. But if in one year after my death, though my executors carefully endeavour to secure such debts, some may be lost, then such bad debt or debts shall be equally shared among my six children, so that no difference in an equal sharing of my movable estate amongst them be; and I do hereby nominate, ordain, institute, and appoint my two sons Robert and Richard Richardson my joint executors of this my last will and testament, revoking all former will or wills by me heretofore made either in word or writing.

In witness whereof I have hereunto set my hand and seal the day and year first above written.

JOHN RICHARDSON. [SEAL.]

Signed sealed published and declared by the testator as his last will and testament in presence of

THOMAS GILPIN,
ABRAHAM DAWES.
JONATHAN RUMFORD.
EDWARD DAWES.

Be it known to all men by these presents whereas I John Richardson of the County of New Castle and Christiana Hundred have made and declared my last will and testament in writing dated the 20th of the 12th month called December 1752 Do ratify and confirm the same with only this further addition, before sharing my movable estate the several legacies be first deducted as is here mentioned.

Item, I give and bequeath to Susanna Bayard wife of Peter Bayard, One Hundred pounds, and to her daughter Elizabeth Rogers, Fifteen Pistoles and to Sarah Finney wife of Jno. Finney One Hundred Pounds, more, and to Rebecca Morris one Hundred Pounds more, and to Hannah Gray Two Hundred Pounds more—And to John Richardson, son to my son Robert, Ten Pistoles and the plantation I live on &c. when at 21 years of age. And my will and meaning is that this codicil be adjudged to be part of my last will and as full and ample in every respect as if the same were so declared and set down in my last will and testament (as above), and to be paid in one year after my death, by my executors as above said.

As witness my hand and seal the 6th day of August in the year of our Lord One Thousand Seven Hundred fifty five (1755).

JOHN RICHARDSON. [SEAL.]

Signed sealed &c. in presence of
  THOMAS GILPIN
  JONATHAN RUMFORD
  EDWARD DAWES

In estimating the value of John Richardsons estate, I have the following data on which to rely, in addition to his will:—viz—Received Christiana November 15th 1759 of Robt. & Rich. Richardson Executors of the Estate of Jno. Richardson decd. the sum of Two Thousand four hundred & Seventy eight Pounds, Eleven Shillings, seven pence in bonds & mortgages, and the further sum of Two Thousand four hundred & thirteen pounds, nine shillings and four pence in cash, together with Two Hundred & seventy six Pounds, sixteen shillings, formerly paid by the executors, which make in the whole the sum of Five

Thousand One hundred & Sixty eight Pounds, Sixteen shillings and eleven pence, being in full for the one sixth part of the deceased personal estate, agreeably to a decree settled in Chancery Oct. 29, 1759.

WILLIAM ARMSTRONG.

Copy from the original in my possession.

Wm. Armstrong married Ann Richardson.

		£	s	d
One sixth being £5168. 16. 11, will make the whole of his residuary estate, given in equal parts to six of his children, amt. to		£31,013.	1.	6
Legacies to his married daughters		1,303.	0.	0
Do to his grandchildren 95 pistoles at £1 8s Penn. Currency		133.		
		£32,446.	6.	1
Valueing the £ at $2.66, Penn. Currency =		$86,306.		

The real estate it is not possible to estimate, but from his will it must have amounted to six or eight hundred acres of land, exclusive of his property in the town of New Castle. But he states in his will that his property was "chiefly personal." Land then was very cheap. This was considered a large estate in that day.

ANN ASHTON, the wife of John Richardson the second, was the daughter of Robert and Elizabeth Ashton; she was born at a place called Elin, in Lincolnshire, England, 8th mo. 5, 1680. Robert Ashton and his family emigrated in company with a number of Friends. They sailed from Hull on the 8th of the 3d mo. 1686, in a ship named the Shoveld, John Howell being master; they landed at New Castle in the 5th mo. following. Soon after

that event, Robert Ashton purchased a large tract of
land of William Penn, on St. George's Creek. His
daughter Sarah married Bartholomew Wyatt, of Salem County, N. J., in 1696. They had two children,
Bartholomew and Elizabeth. The first, born 1st mo.
4th, 1697, married Elizabeth Tomlinson, of Haddon-
field, N. J.; and Elizabeth, born 7th mo. 16, 1706,
married Robert Smith. The Wyatts intermarried
with the Wistar family of Philadelphia. See Thomas
Shoards's book, entitled "Fenwick's Colony," 1877;
he obtained the information from the Records of Salem
Monthly Meeting, &c. Tradition says John Richardson 2d emigrated in the same ship. This is doubtful,
though he might not have come with his father, who
is believed to have emigrated in 1682, when the 2d
John was but four years old.

Ann Ashton was married to John Richardson 7th
mo. 7th, 1701. She is represented as being a most
excellent woman, remarkable for her benevolence and
kindness of heart, particularly to the poor and sick,
riding about the neighborhood with necessaries to
distribute among them. She died 4th mo. 18, 1748,
aged 67 years, 8 months, 13 days; her husband survived her more than seven years. The Ashtons or
Asshetons were natives of Bristol, England, or its
vicinity, and cousins of Wm. Penn; part of the family
became converts to the Society of Friends, while others
remained members of the Church of England. Robert
Ashton, the father of Ann, was a Quaker. Robert
Ashton of Philadelphia, of the same family, was a

member of the Episcopal Church, and held several important offices in Pennsylvania under Penn's Government. He has descendants in Philadelphia at this day. He is interred in the ground attached to Christ Church, in Second Street, Philadelphia.

THIRD GENERATION.

ELIZABETH RICHARDSON, daughter and first child of John and Ann Richardson, was born at the family residence on Christiana Creek 9th mo. 4, 1705, and died the 15th of 1st month, 1734, aged 28 years, 9 months, 6 days, unmarried.

JOSEPH RICHARDSON, son and second child of John and Ann Richardson, was born at the family residence on Christiana Creek, 10th mo. 6, 1706. Married Sarah Morris, daughter of William Morris, of Trenton, N. J., and sister of William Morris, Jr., who married his sister Rebecca in 1744, and died in Philadelphia 11th mo. 17th, 1770, aged 64 years, 1 month, 11 days.

His wife died in about a year after their marriage, soon after the birth of their daughter Sarah Richardson, aged about 20 years. He never married a second time.

In his younger days, in connection with his father's business, he acquired a knowledge and taste for mercantile affairs, making frequent voyages to the West Indies, in charge of the cargo. His father, during his absence on one of the voyages, built a house for him, at the place mentioned in his will as "Snug Harbor," about half a mile further up the Christiana

Creek than his own residence. Upon Joseph's return, he declined living in it, stating his determination to settle in Philadelphia. The house had then progressed so far as to be roofed in, but was never finished, and was known in the neighborhood as " Richardson's Folly," or the " Folly House," and from this circumstance the " Folly Woods" near by obtained its name. The cellar and foundations were to be seen until they were excavated by the Philadelphia, Wilmington, and Baltimore R. R. Co., their road passing over the site. Joseph carried out his intention of settling in Philadelphia, and, as a merchant there, acquired a large fortune by successful industry.

He built the house now standing at Nos. 256 and 258 South Second Street, in Philadelphia, and died there; it stands back a considerable distance from Second Street, with an office and side yard, and fronting on Second Street, in its original condition.

ROBERT RICHARDSON, second son and third child of John and Elizabeth Richardson, was born at his father's residence 5th mo. 31, 1708, married Sarah Shipley 10th mo. 6, 1750, and died 6mo. 18, 1761, aged 53 years 18 days. Sarah, the wife of Robert Richardson, was born 5th mo. 25, 1729, died 6mo. 28, 1793, aged 64 years, 1 month, 3 days. They had four children, Elizabeth, Mary, John, and Ann Richardson.

In his early life Robert Richardson was connected with the shipping business with his father, and inherited most of the real estate of his parents on the

Christiana, excepting that part left to his son John. After his marriage, he resided in Wilmington, engaged in the mercantile business; had his place of business at the foot of Orange Street, resided on the hill on West Street between Third and Fourth Streets. After the death of his father, in 1755, he removed to the old family mansion on Christiana Creek. He was about removing to Philadelphia when he died.

Sarah Richardson, the wife of Robert Richardson, was the daughter of Wm. Shipley, one of the founders of Wilmington, and his second wife, Elizabeth, the daughter of Samuel Levis, of Springfield, Chester (now Delaware Co.), Pennsylvania. Elizabeth Shipley was an eminent minister in the Society of Friends at that day, and on her death-bed, in 1777, just after the battle of Brandywine and the capture of Philadelphia, when all chances seemed against it, prophesied the success of the Americans, and the achievement of their independence.* Wm. Shipley removed to Wilmington in 1736. His wife Elizabeth, at the time of her death, was 87 years old, having been a minister 63 years.

SUSANNAH RICHARDSON, daughter and fourth child of John and Ann Richardson, was born at the family mansion 9th mo. 19, 1710, married Peter Bayard, of Bohemia, Maryland (date not known), and died 11th mo. 26, 1766, aged 56 years, 3 months, 7

* See B. Ferris's "Original Settlements on the Delaware," p. 258.

'days. The time of her husband's death is unknown.
Their children were Elizabeth, Ann, Susannah, and
John R. Bayard.

SARAH RICHARDSON, daughter and fifth child of
John and Ann Richardson, was born at the family
mansion 7th mo. 9, 1712, married to Dr. John Finney
about 1742, and died 8th mo. 15, 1772, aged 60 years,
1 month, 6 days. The time of Dr. Finney's birth is
not known. He died 3d mo. 22, 1774. They had four
children, none of whom survived their parents. The
following inscription is found on a head-stone in our
family lot, in Friends' burying-ground, New Castle.
"Here lies deposited the body of John, son of Dr.
Jno. Finney, Esq., and Sarah his wife, who departed
this life the 19th of January, 1753, aged 4 years and
2 months. Also, the remains of his three brothers,
who died in their infancy." Tradition says Sarah
Finney was the beauty and belle of that generation
of the family.

ANN RICHARDSON, fourth daughter and sixth child
of Jno. and Ann Richardson, was born at the family
mansion 5th mo. 1, 1714, married Col. Wm. Armstrong
about 1758, and died 2d mo. 20, 1799, aged 84 years,
9 months, 8 days. They had no children. They
owned and resided on the property since belonging to
Wm. Armor, and more recently to the late Samuel
Canby, in Christiana Hundred, New Castle Co., near
Brandywine Springs. After her husband's death she

resided in Wilmington, to the time of her death, on the east side of Shipley, about half way between Third and Fourth Streets. Wm. Armstrong was a member of the legislature of the State of Delaware for the years 1742-3-4-5, and probably oftener. (*See American Weekly Mercury* for those years.) The time of his birth and death is not known. He was alive in 1775.

MARY RICHARDSON, fifth daughter and seventh child of John and Ann Richardson, was born at the family mansion 12th mo. 22, 1715, and married Peter Reeve in Philadelphia, in the spring of 1772. Being Friends, they were both disowned for marrying out of the Society by the Philadelphia Monthly Meeting. She died 11th mo. 18, 1798, aged 82 years, 10 months, 15 days. They had no children. They resided in Spruce Street, Philadelphia, now No. 336, and owned by Deborah Wharton. Peter Reeve had been a sea-captain, and survived his wife a few years, being 80 years old at the time of his death. His will was proved Oct. 24, 1800: in it he leaves many legacies; among them he desires " my niece Sarah Waln (only child of Joseph Richardson), to accept £10, to purchase a piece of plate in remembrance of her many kindnesses to me."

She removed from Delaware to Philadelphia about 1767, living with her brother Joseph, after the death of his wife, until his decease, after which she married late in life.

REBECCA RICHARDSON, sixth daughter and eighth child of John and Ann Richardson, was born at the family mansion 6th mo. 22, 1717; married twice, first to Joseph Peters, son of Thomas Peters, of Philadelphia, 2d mo. 13, 1741. Marriage certificate recorded in book marriages of Newark (now Kennet) Monthly Meeting. He came to Wilmington by certificate of removal, from Philadelphia Monthly Meeting, 29th 6th mo., 1740, and was disowned by Newark Monthly Meeting, for arming a merchant vessel, 10th mo. 3, 1748. He carried on the mercantile business in Wilmington. The date of his death is not known, but he was alive 2d mo. 11, 1746, and advertised in the "Penna. Gazette" the following: "Lately imported from London, in the ship Caroline, Capt. Mesnard, and sold by Joseph Peters, of Wilmington, by wholesale or retail, very reasonable, for ready money, or short credit." (Here follows a long list of goods, of great variety.)

Her second husband, William Morris, was a native of Trenton, N. J., son of William Morris, and grandson of Anthony Morris, of Philadelphia. They were married in Friends meeting, at Wilmington, 10th mo. 5, 1752. His sister, Sarah Morris, married her brother, Joseph Richardson, in 1744.

Wm. Morris was also in the mercantile business at Trenton, and afterwards at Wilmington. He and his wife resided at the southeast corner of Market and Front Street, in that city. He advertised in the "Penna. Gazette," 1746, viz.: "To be sold by Wm.

5

Morris, Jr., at his store in Trenton, good rum by the hogshead, and salt by the 100 bushels, or less quantity, at Philadelphia price, and freight up from thence." She died in Wilmington 11th mo. 23, 1773, age 56 years, 5 months, 1 day. The date of her husband's decease is not known. She had no children by either marriage.

JOHN RICHARDSON, third son and ninth child of John and Ann Richardson, was born at the family mansion 10th mo. 6, 1718, and died 4th mo. 18, 1737, unmarried. He was assisting Wm. Empson, a neighbor, to raise a barn, and was killed by the falling of a piece of timber.

RICHARD RICHARDSON, fourth son and tenth child of John and Ann Richardson, was born at the family mansion 6th mo. 9th, 1720. Married Sarah Tatnall, daughter of Edward and Elizabeth Tatnall, of Wilmington, and granddaughter of Joseph and Mary Pennock, of Marlborough, Chester Co., Pennsylvania, 4th mo. 24, 1766, at Friends meeting in Wilmington. He died 9th mo. 10, 1797, aged 77 years, 2 months, 20 days.

Sarah, his wife, was born at Wilmington, 8th mo. 31, 1745, and died there at the corner of French and Third Streets, 9th mo. 6, 1834, aged 89 years, 5 days. She survived her husband 37 years, resided with her daughter Ann, in Wilmington, after her husband's death. Richard resided, previous to and at the time of his marriage, in the brick house now standing near the Baltimore Road, 1½ miles from Wilmington, and near the bridge over Mill Creek, his sister Jane living with him, and keeping house for him during his single life. He carried on the milling business, in a mill that stood between the aforesaid brick house and the road; it formerly belonged to his father, and which, with the land there, he inherited of him; also, had a bakery, at which he manufactured ship bread. This mill was standing, the machinery having been removed, within my recollection, some of it remaining until about 1835 or 1836, or later; it was a one-storied building, with basement and loft, hip-roofed, with an overshot wheel of 12 or 14 feet.

The first mill ever constructed on Mill Creek was of the kind called a tub, having the water-wheel, which was horizontal, at one end of a perpendicular shaft, and the mill-stone at the other, situated further up the creek, near where Stidham's Run comes in, and was propelled by the force of the running water, without much if any dam. It originally belonged to four persons, one-third to Jonas and Gisbert Walraven, one-third to John Sinexson, and the other third to John Richardson, who purchased the other two-thirds in 1723 for £13 each, or $69.16 for both shares, which also included 17 acres of land. At this primitive mill, the person in charge was in the habit of putting five or six bushels of corn in the hopper in the morning, set the machine in motion, then go to his ploughing or other work, returning at noon to give it another supply.

The upper stone had a pin projecting upwards from its surface, which, with every revolution, shook a few grains from the shoe into the stones to be ground.

The second mill, before referred to, would now also be regarded as a pretty simple affair. The tide then flowing into Mill Creek ascended as high as the mill, which was at its head, the creek being navigable for small vessels, thus affording facilities for bringing grain and grists by water. The bolting of meal was done by hand, and I have heard my father say, that when a boy, he used to be set to turn the bolting cloth, and when becoming tired and vexed with the job, whirled it round so fast as to send the flour out at the end of the cloth with the bran, and it had to be done over again. At the time of the Revolutionary War, a regiment of American soldiers encamped on the opposite side of the creek, just previous to the battle of Brandywine, often visited the mill, and being mischievously disposed, would throw chunks of fat pork, part of their rations, into the eye of the millstones, to be ground up with the grain, saying, as an apology, that "the mill wanted grease," thereby spoiling the meal. These soldiers also stole everything they could lay their hands on, in the shape of eatables: robbing the orchards, hen-roosts, and gardens: taking the pies and bread out of the oven on baking days, and were so troublesome about the house day and night, that my grandfather offered the officer in command a bed to lodge in the house, which he accepted, and it had the effect to keep them away at night. There used to be,

and probably is yet, the mark where a musket ball
was shot through the kitchen door by one of these
soldiers, because they refused to let him in at night.
As it was expected that the battle of Brandywine
would be fought in this vicinity, after the landing of
Gen. Howe at Elkton, being in the direct course to
Philadelphia, my grandfather and his family removed
to Marlborough, in Chester Co., for safety, thereby
putting themselves immediately in the route of the
British army, which they had attempted to avoid.
The present grain mill was built by my grandfather
in the year 1785, and the old one abandoned : he also
built the present saw mill, as well as the fine old sub-
stantial stone house on the same premises, and which
will compare favorably with any other in its neighborhood. It was built in 1765, and has stood more
than one hundred years, and looks as though it might
stand another hundred with little damage. It, with
the mills and property there, is now owned by his
grandson, Samuel Richardson. His children were
Joseph, John, Elizabeth, Richard, Ashton, Ann, and
John Richardson.

HANNAH RICHARDSON, seventh daughter and
eleventh child of John and Ann Richardson, was born
at the family mansion 9th mo. 16, 1721, and was
married twice, first to Thomas Gray about 1751 or
1752, and the second time to Francis Johnson ; the
time of this marriage I am unable to fix. She was
his wife in 1766; how much sooner is not known.

As regards her first marriage, her father says in his will, made in the 12th mo. 1752, that she was "lately married to Thos. Gray," from whence I get the date above.

Gray probably died some time between "Oct. 1756" and "March, 1759," as he signed a receipt at the first date for part of his wife's legacy, and she herself at the latter date for the other part of it. But this is not positive proof of his being dead at that time.

She died 11th mo. 11, 1787, aged 66 years, 1 month, 14 days. She had no children by either marriage.

JANE RICHARDSON, eighth daughter and twelfth child of John and Ann Richardson, was born at the family mansion 2d mo. 1, 1727, married Dr. John McKinley between 1761 and 1766, and died 7th mo. 18, 1805, suddenly, whilst sitting in her chair, in apparent good health, by apoplexy or paralysis, at the age of 78 years, 5 months, 17 days. They had no children. They resided in Wilmington, northwest corner of French and Third Streets. Her husband was the first Governor (or President) of the State of Delaware, appointed 2d mo. 1777, after the Declaration of Independence. He was taken from his bed by the British on the night of the 11th of the 9th mo. 1777, the day after the battle of Brandywine; his desk broken open, and all his papers taken. From letters to his wife, still extant, it appears he was carried to New Castle and confined in the Solbay, a war vessel. He continued on board until the British captured

Philadelphia and obtained possession of the forts on the Delaware, when he was removed, 11th mo. 22d, to a prison ship at Chester, and from thence to Philadelphia; where he was imprisoned in the State House in that city until the English evacuated it, on the 16th of the 6th mo. 1778. He was taken with them by sea to New York, and confined at Flatbush, on Long Island, until, in the following month, he was paroled and returned to Philadelphia; where, after some delay on the part of Congress, he was exchanged in the 9th month, and returned to his home and family, after a captivity of about a year.

He is interred in the Presbyterian churchyard, corner of Market and Tenth Streets, Wilmington. On his tombstone there is inscribed: "This monument is erected in memory of John McKinley, M.D., who was born in the Kingdom of Ireland on the 24th of February, A. D. 1721, and died in this town on the 31st of August, A. D. 1796. He settled early in life in this country, and pursuing the practice of physic, soon became eminent in his profession. He served in several important public employments, and, particularly, was the first person that filled the office of President of the State, after the Declaration of Independence. He died full of years, having passed a long life usefully to the public, and honorably to himself." His wife was interred in the ground at New Castle.

FOURTH GENERATION.

CHILDREN OF JOSEPH AND SARAH RICHARDSON.

SARAH RICHARDSON. only child of J. and S. Richardson. was born in Philadelphia. 8th mo. 22, 1746. married Nicholas, son of Nicholas and Mary Waln, 5th mo. 22, 1771, and died in Philadelphia 4th mo. 13, 1825, aged 78 years. 7 months. 22 days. Being her father's only child. she inherited a large estate.

Nicholas Waln was born at Fairhill. near Philadelphia, 9th mo. 19, 1742; he was an eminent lawyer in his early life, but taking a religious turn, he abandoned the profession, and became a prominent minister in the Society of Friends. He died at their home, now Nos. 256 and 258 South Second Street, Philadelphia (which had been the residence of his wife's parents), 9th mo. 29, 1813, aged 71 years, 10 days.

I remember Sarah Waln, the oldest member of the family of whom I had any knowledge. She was a small, thin old lady, with rather masculine features, and great vivacity of manners. Their children were Joseph. William, Nicholas, Mary, and Jacob.

CHILDREN OF ROBERT AND SARAH RICHARDSON.

ELIZABETH RICHARDSON. daughter of R. and S. Richardson, was born in Wilmington, 11th mo. 10, 1751; married Charles Wharton, of Philadelphia, son of Joseph and Hannah Wharton, 10th mo. 22, 1778: and died in Philadelphia 5th mo. 22, 1782, aged 30 years, 6 months, 12 days, leaving no children.

JOHN RICHARDSON, son of Robert and Sarah Richardson, was born 10th mo. 23, 1753, and died at his farm, on the Newport Road, 2½ miles from Wilmington, which he inherited from his grandfather, when he was a child about 18 months old. On the night of the 23d of 11th mo. 1800, he was found dead in his bed; having died of apoplexy, as was supposed, at the age of 47 years, 1 month. This property now belongs to Henry Latimer, his nephew. He died unmarried.

MARY RICHARDSON, daughter of R. and S. Richardson, was born in Wilmington, 3d mo. 10, 1758, and died there 9th mo. 7, 1795; age 37 years, 5 months, 28 days. Unmarried.

ANN RICHARDSON, daughter of Robert and Sarah Richardson, was born in Wilmington, 8th mo. 3, 1760: married Dr. Henry Latimer, of Wilmington, 2d mo. 26, 1789; died in that city, on the west side of Market Street between Fifth and Sixth Streets, 11th mo. 6, 1838; age 78 years, 3 months, 3 days.

Dr. Latimer was born 4th mo. 24, 1752, and died 12th mo. 19, 1819, aged 67 years, 7 months, 25 days. Interred in the Presbyterian churchyard, Market and Tenth Street, Wilmington, where there is a tombstone over his remains. Their children were Sarah, John R., Mary R., Henry, and James Latimer.

CHILDREN OF PETER AND SUSANNAH BAYARD.

ANN BAYARD, daughter of Peter and Susannah
Bayard. The dates of her birth and death are not
known. Married a person by the name of Scott; time
unknown. But one child, Martha Scott.

JOHN R. BAYARD, born 1739, died 1756, age 17.
Unmarried.

SUSANNAH BAYARD, date of birth and death unknown. Married Jonathan Smith: date not known.
Children, John, Mary, Samuel, and Susannah Smith.

ELIZABETH BAYARD, date of birth and death not
known. Married John Rogers about 1752. Mentioned in her grandfather John Richardson's will, who
left her a legacy: her name was then Rogers.
They had two children, Dr. John R. B. Rogers,
and a daughter whose name is not known, who married Rev. Dr. Tennant. John Rogers, the husband of
Eliz. Bayard, was born at Boston, N. E., 8th mo. 5,
1727, and died 5th mo. 7, 1811, in his 84th year. His
parents came from Londonderry, Ireland, 1721, and removed to Philadelphia, 1728. He was converted by the
preaching of Whitefield, on the court-house steps at
night in Philadelphia: passing near the place, he stop-
ped to hear, and held a lantern for his accommodation;
absorbed and deeply interested in the discourse, the
lantern fell from his hands, and was dashed to pieces.

When little more than twelve years old he became hopefully pious. He was a noted minister in the Presbyterian Church, and joined in the division in that church in that day, in Pennsylvania, and became one of Tennant's party or "New Side." (*See* a Biographical account of him in Webster's History of the Presbyterian Church in America, page 576.)

CHILDREN OF RICHARD AND SARAH RICHARDSON.

JOSEPH RICHARDSON, eldest son of R. and S. Richardson, was born at Mill Creek, 2d mo. 19, 1767; married Ann Spackman, daughter of George and Thomazin Spackman, of Wilmington, at Friends' meeting there, 6th mo. 16, 1803; and deceased at his residence 12th mo. 24th, 1833, aged 66 years, 10 months, 5 days; buried in Friends' ground, Wilmington. He inherited the property at Mill Creek, and resided there all his life. His wife was born 12th mo. 28, 1777, and died in Wilmington, 6th mo. 23, 1842, aged 64 years, 5 months, 26 days, and is interred in the Friends' ground there. Children, Jane, Samuel S., Sarah, Thomazin, Edward, Joseph, and George.

JOHN RICHARDSON, son of R. and S. Richardson, born 5th mo. 30, 1769, died 1st mo. 7, 1773, aged 3 years, 7 months, 7 days.

ELIZABETH RICHARDSON, daughter of R. and S. Richardson, was born at Mill Creek, 7th mo. 20, 1771, married Samuel Stroud, son of James Stroud and Ann his wife, of Wilmington, 10th mo. 29, 1789, and died there 11th mo. 5, 1847, aged 76 years, 3 months, 16 days, and is interred in Friends' ground in that city. Her husband died in Wilmington in 1832, and is buried in Friends' ground there. Children, Ann, Mary, Edward, Samuel, Sarah R., and James.

RICHARD RICHARDSON, son of Richard and Sarah Richardson, was born at Mill Creek, 7th mo. 27, 1774, died 12th mo. 6, 1774, aged 5 months, 21 days.

ASHTON RICHARDSON, son of Richard and Sarah Richardson, was born at Mill Creek, 5th mo. 6, 1776. Married Mary Wood, daughter of Robert and Elizabeth Wood, and granddaughter of Joseph and Mary Wood, of Philadelphia, in the Friends' meeting-house that then stood on the south side of Pine Street, below Second in that city, 6th mo. 5, 1807. He died at his residence, Ashley farm, on the Baltimore Road, near the place of his birth, 8th mo. 10, 1852, of disease of the heart, aged 76 years, 3 months, and 4 days, and is interred in the Friends' ground in Wilmington. His wife was born in Philadelphia, 4th mo. 1, 1785, and died at her residence in Delaware, 2d mo. 1, 1853, aged 67 years, 10 months, and is interred alongside of her husband, surviving him less than six months. My father built the house in 1806, in which he resided from the time of his marriage until his death, on land, most of which was purchased from Peter Walraven, which is now the residence of his children, Ashton and Hannah W. Richardson.

His children are Richard, Robert W., Elizabeth, Mary, Sarah, Hannah W., Lucy, and Ashton Richardson, and three others who died in infancy.

ANN RICHARDSON, daughter of Richard and Sarah Richardson, was born at Mill Creek, 10th mo. 20, 1778, and died, unmarried, 7th mo. 9, 1845, aged 66 years, 8 months, 19 days, at the residence of her brother Ashton. She resided in Wilmington with her mother after the death of her father, and continued to live there, keeping house by herself after her mother's death, in 1832, being only temporarily at her brother's at the time of her decease. She is interred in Wilmington in the Friends' ground, in the family row.

JOHN RICHARDSON, son of Richard and Sarah Richardson, was born at Mill Creek, 5th mo. 18, 1783, married Margaret Paxson, daughter of Joseph Paxson, and Sarah his wife, 5th mo. 11, 1813, and died in Wilmington, 9th mo. 30, 1859, aged 76 years, 4 months, 12 days, and is interred in the Friends' ground, Wilmington, in the family row. He resided most of his life at Rockwell farm, near the place of his birth, building the house he occupied there, soon after his marriage, now belonging to his son John. His children are Sarah T., Anna, William P., Elizabeth, Mary, John, and Joseph P. Richardson.

FIFTH GENERATION.

CHILDREN OF NICHOLAS AND SARAH WALN.

Joseph R., b.　　　1770; d.　　　1782; age 12 yrs.
William. b.　　　1775; d.　　　1825; age 50 yrs.; m. 1805.
　　Mary Wilcox. Five children.
Nicholas, b.　　　1778; d. 7 mo. 4, 1849; age 71. Unmarried.
Mary. b.　　　: d. in infancy.
Jacob S., b. 8 mo. 19, 1783; d. 6 mo. 30, 1847; age 63 yrs., 10 mos.,
　　11 da. Unmarried.

CHILDREN OF DR. HENRY AND ANN LATIMER.

Sarah, b.　　　: d.　　　1828; age　　. Unmarried.
John R., b. 12 mo. 10, 1793; d. 1 mo. 18, 1865; age 71 yrs., 1 mo.,
　　8 da.; m. 7 mo.　　　1834. Elizabeth Kepley, of Philadelphia.
　　No children.
Mary R., b. 7 mo. 29, 1796; d. 2 mo. 8, 1871; age 74 yrs., 6 mos.,
　　9 da. Unmarried.
Henry, b. 5 mo. 21, 1799; d.　　　: m. 6 mo. 6, 1822. Sarah
　　Ann Baily, daughter of Jos. and Elizabeth Baily. Six children.
James, b. 1 mo. 26, 1802; d.　　　1837; age 35 yrs. Unmarried.

CHILD OF ——— SCOTT AND ANN SCOTT.

Martha, b. not known: d. not known. She committed suicide when
young, caused by an unrequited love affair.

CHILDREN OF JONATHAN AND SUSANNA SMITH.

John R.,
Mary.
Samuel.
Susanna.
　　Nothing further known of this branch.

CHILDREN OF JOHN AND ELIZABETH ROGERS.

John R. B., date of birth and death not known. No children.

Susanna, date of birth and death not known; m. Dr. William Tennant. Children, if any, not known.

CHILDREN OF JOSEPH AND ANN S. RICHARDSON.

Jane, b. 6 mo. 5, 1805; d. 9 mo. 11, 1839; age 34 yrs. 3 mos., 6 da.;
m. 6 mo. 15, 1837. Sam. S. Poole, son of Wm. and Sarah Poole,
of Wilmington. No children.

Samuel S., b. 10 mo. 11, 1806; d.   ; m. 10 mo. 14, 1841.
Susan, daughter of Wm. and Elizabeth Robinson, of Wilmington.
Six children. His wife died 7 mo.   1865.

Sarah, b. 2 mo. 4, 1808; d. 12 mo. 25, 1839; age 31 yrs., 10 mos.,
21 da. Unmarried.

Thomazin, b. 11 mo. 26, 1810; d.

Edward T., b. 6 mo. 7, 1812; d. 2 mo. 19, 1877; age 64 yrs., 6 mos.,
12 da.; m. 5 mo. 20, 1841. Hannah Masden. No children.

Joseph, b. 10 mo. 12, 1814.

George, b. 1 mo. 29, 1816; d.   ; m. 3 mo. 13, 1845. Sarah,
daughter of Jno. and Susan Woolston. Three children. His
wife died 12 mo. 31, 1877.

CHILDREN OF SAMUEL AND ELIZABETH STROUD.

Ann, b. 12 mo. 16, 1795; d.   ; m. 12 mo. 16, 1820. Stephen
Pancoast, of Delaware Co., Pa. Six children. Her husband
died 12 mo. 15, 1873, in Philadelphia.

Mary, b. 9 mo. 21, 1797; d. 4 mo. 20, 1821; age 23 yrs., 6 mos., 29
da.; m. 3 mo. 29, 1819. Stephen Bonsall, of Wilmington. No
children.

Edward, b. 1 mo. 19, 1800; d.   1821. Unmarried. Died
of yellow fever at Havanna.

Samuel, b. 1 mo. 20, 1803; d. 8 mo. 31, 1866; age 63 yrs., 7 mos.,
11 da.; m. 5 mo. 5, 1827. Mary E., daughter of Wm. Jones, of
Wilmington. Five children.

Sarah R., b. 6 mo. 21, 1806; d. 6 mo. 29, 1875; age 69 yrs., 8 da.;
m. 11 mo. 4, 1830, Jesse, son of Eli and Phebe Mendinhall, of
Wilmington. Five children. Her husband died 11 mo. 15. 1852.
James. b. 8 mo. 23. 1811; d.   : m. 2 mo. 16. 1835. Hannah
Ford Hedges, daughter of John and Elizabeth Hedges. of Wilmington. Eight children. His wife died 12 mo. 24, 1863; age
51 yrs.. 1 mo.. 11 da.

CHILDREN OF ASHTON AND MARY RICHARDSON.

Richard. b. 4 mo. 18. 1808; m. 8 mo. 12, 1841. Hannah, daughter of
Josiah and Elizabeth White, of Philadelphia. No children.
Robert W., b. 7 mo. 6. 1810; d. 1 mo. 7. 1869; age 58 yrs., 6 mos..
1 da.; m. 6 mo. 17. 1847. Elizabeth R.. daughter of Sam. and
Mary Hulme. of Bristol. Pa. No children.
Elizabeth. b. 8 mo. 28. 1812; d. 6 mo. 14, 1867: age 54 yrs.. 9 mos..
16 da.: m. 5 mo. 14. 1835. William. son of William and Mary
Hodgson. of Philadelphia. Two children.
Mary. b. 2 mo. 20. 1815: d.   : m. 6 mo. 21. 1867. Thomas,
son of Thomas and Mary Wistar. of Philadelphia. No children.
Her husband died 1 mo. 16. 1876.
Sarah. b. 4 mo. 5. 1817; d. 4 mo. 11. 1876: age 59 yrs.. 6 da.; m. 6
mo. 10. 1841. Joseph. son of Edw. and Margery Tatnall. of Wil-
mington. Twelve children.
Hannah W.. b. 5 mo. 23. 1819; d.
Lucy. b. 11 mo. 23. 1824: d.   : m. 4 mo. 15. 1852. John
R.. son of Jno. W. and Mary Tatum. of Wilmington. Six chil-
dren.
Ashton. b. 2 mo. 21. 1830: d.

CHILDREN OF JOHN AND MARGARET RICHARDSON.

Sarah T.. b. 2 mo. 15. 1815; d. 6 mo. 18. 1861: age 46 yrs.. 4 mos..
3 da.: m. 1 mo. 24. 1856. Edward T.. son of John and Ann Bellach.
No children.

Anna, b. 8 mo. 11, 1816; d.   ; m. 10 mo. 6, 1842, Joseph,
son of Joseph and Deborah Bringhurst, of Wilmington. Three
children.

William P., b. 7 mo. 11, 1818; d.   ; m. 2 mo. 16, 1865.
Mary W. Forst, daughter of Joseph and Elizabeth Warner, of
Bristol, Pa. No children.

Elizabeth, b. 5 mo. 19, 1819; d.   ; m. 11 mo. 9, 1853,
Joseph C., son of John and Tabitha Turnpenny, of Philadelphia.
No children.

Mary, b. 12 mo. 31, 1821; d.   ; m. 6 mo. 22, 1843, Charles,
son of Wm. and Esther Warner, of Wilmington. Two children.

John, b. 2 mo. 2, 1824; d.   ; m. 6 mo. 12, 1856, Martha,
daughter of John and Sarah Andrews, of Darby, Pa. Three
children.

Joseph P., b. 12 mo. 16, 1825; d.   ; m. 11 mo. 13, 1856,
Sarah, daughter of John and Sarah Andrews, of Darby, Pa.
Seven children.

SIXTH GENERATION.

CHILDREN OF WILLIAM AND MARY WALN.

John. b.   ; d.   . Unmarried.

Sarah. b.   ; d.   ; m.   Benjamin C.
    Wilcox.   children.

Nicholas. b.   ; died   unmarried.

William. b.   ; d.   ; m.

Mary. b.   ; d.   ; m.   Dr.   Maxwell.
    children.

CHILDREN OF HENRY AND SARAH ANN LATIMER.

Elizabeth. b.

Henry. b.

Anna. b.

Joseph B.. b.   ; d.   1860.

John. b.

Mary. b.   None married.

Descendants of the children of Jonathan and Susanna Smith. if any.
not known.

Descendants of Dr. William and Susanna Tennant. if any. not
known.

CHILDREN OF SAMUEL AND SUSAN RICHARDSON.

Ann S.. b. 9 mo. 27, 1843; d.   ; m. 9 mo. 28, 1871, John
    Sellers Bancroft.   Two children.

Elizabeth R., b. 9 mo. 18, 1845; d. 3 mo. 5, 1869; age 23 yrs.. 5 mos.,
    18 da.; m. 10 mo. 23, 1866, John Sellers Bancroft.   Two children.

Mary A., b. 2 mo. 15, 1817; d.   ; m.   1865, Samuel
    Bancroft. Two children.

Jane, b. 1 mo. 21, 1819; d.   ; m. 10 mo, 13, 1870, Joshua
    Pusey. Two children.

Lucy J., b. 4 mo. 12, 1851; d.   ; m. 10 mo. 8, 1872, Gilbert
    Cameron. Two children.

Joseph, b. 1 mo. 1, 1854; d.   ; m.

CHILDREN OF GEORGE AND SARAH W. RICHARDSON.

Henry B., b. 1 mo. 10, 1846; d. 1 mo. 2, 1876; age 30 yrs., 2 mos.,
    22 da.; m.   Sarah Speakman. Two children.

Susan W., b. 2 mo. 7, 1848; d.

Joseph A., b. 7 mo. 13, 1849; d.

CHILDREN OF STEPHEN AND ANN PANCOAST.

Mary Stroud, b. 11 mo. 1, 1821; d.   ; m.

Seth, b. 7 mo. 28, 1823; d.   ; m. 1st, 1 mo. 6, 1853, Sarah
    S. Osborn. Three children. His wife d. 1 mo. 3, 1868. M. 2d.
    1 mo. 11, 1869, Susan G, Osborn. Three children. His 2d wife
    d. 12 mo. 16, 1876.

Elizabeth Stroud, b. 1 mo. 25, 1825; d.   ; m.

Sarah Richardson, b. 12 mo. 28, 1826; d.   ; m.

Abigail, b. 7 mo. 16, 1828; d. 11 mo. 6. 1859. Unmarried. Age 31
    yrs., 3 mos., 20 da.

Anna, b. 7 mo. 31, 1830; d. 3 mo. 24, 1864; age 33 yrs., 7 mos., 24
    da.; m. 12 mo. 17, 1857, Henry Halderman. Two children. Her
    husband died 1 mo. 13, 1866.

CHILDREN OF SAMUEL AND MARY E. STROUD.

Edward, b. 3 mo. 23, 1830; d.   ; m. 3 mo. 13, 1856, Mary
    E. Reynolds. Six children.

William J., b. 9 mo. 1, 1836; d.   : m. 3 mo. 13. 1862, Clara
    E. Pennington. Six children.

Ann Elizabeth, b. 7 mo. 30, 1838; d.   ; m.

Hannah J., b. 2 mo. 26, 1841; d.   ; m. 5 mo. 5, 1865, Alfred
    Gawthrop. Four children.

Mary. b. 5 mo. 3, 1843; d. 9 mo. 1, 1846. Unmarried.

CHILDREN OF JESSE AND SARAH R. MENDINHALL.

Elizabeth S., b. 9 mo. 8, 1831; d.   ; m. 7 mo. 12, 1854,
    T. Clarkson Taylor. Six children.

Edward. b. 2 mo. 29, 1834: d.   ; m. 1 mo. 7, 1858, Lydia
    S. Marshall. Four children.

Henry. b. 8 mo. 26, 1837; d.   ; m. 9 mo. 11, 1860,
    Elizabeth W. Wilson. Two children.

Mary S., b. 5 mo. 22, 1841; d.   ; m. 5 mo. 20, 1863,
    Granville Worrell. Three children.

William G., b. 6 mo. 26, 1845.

CHILDREN OF JAMES AND HANNAH F. STROUD.

Elizabeth Thornton. b. 4 mo. 22, 1836; d.   ; m. 2 mo. 28,
    1861. George W. Scarborough. Five children.

William Penn. b. 1 mo. 3, 1838; d.   ; m. 12 mo. 20, 1866,
    Mary H. Towers. No children.

Mary Bonsall. b. 2 mo. 15, 1840; d. 1 mo. 9, 1869; age 28 yrs., 10
    mos., 25 da.; m. 5 mo. 20, 1866, John C. Piel. Two children.

Charles Franklin. b. 2 mo. 15, 1842: d.   ; m. 9 mo. 10,
    1867, Fanny Roche. Three children.

John Hedges, b. 9 mo. 6, 1844; d.   ; m. 8 mo. 29, 1867,
    Emma T. A. Fœring. One child.

Adeline Ella, b. 10 mo. 1, 1847; d. 9 mo. 3, 1870; m.   .
    James C. Wilson. Two children.

James. b. 12 mo. 4, 1850; d. 6 mo. 14, 1851.

Sally Iva. b. 2 mo. 2, 1853: d.   ; m. 2 mo. 9, 1875,
    Jonathan Thomas Purcel. One child.

CHILDREN OF WILLIAM AND ELIZABETH R. HODGSON.

Mary R., b. 4 mo. 30, 1836; d.   ; m. 7 mo. 5, 1871, Henry
 Albertson.   Three children.
Anna, b. 5 mo. 11, 1838; d.

CHILDREN OF JOSEPH AND SARAH R. TATNALL.

Edward, b. 11mo. 10, 1842; d. 1 mo. 18, 1878; age 35 yrs., 2 mos..
  8 da.; m. 6 mo. 21, 1866, Rachel Alsop.   Two children.
Ann W., b. 4 mo. 22, 1844; d. 11 mo. 21, 1859; age 15 yrs.. 6 mos..
  29 da. Unmarried.
Mary R., b. 12 mo. 30, 1845; d. 6 mo. 29. 1872; age 26 yrs., 5 mos..
  28 da.; m. 10 mo. 16, 1868, Robert Brown.   Two children.
Elizabeth, b. 9 mo. 29, 1847; d. 1 mo. 19. 1874; age 26 yrs.. 3 mos..
  21 da.; m. 2 mo. 17, 1870, John R. Bringhurst.   Two children.
Joseph, b. 5 mo. 31, 1849; d.   ; m.
Ashton R., b. 11 mo. 11, 1850; d.   ; m. 11 mo. 15, 1877.
 Mary Reybold.
Thomas, b. 12 mo. 2, 1852.
Richard R., b. 12 mo. 2, 1856.
Lucy, b. 12 mo. 2, 1856.
Samuel, b. 12 mo. 1857; d.
Robert R., b. 2 mo. 20, 1859; d.   1859: age
William, b. 1 mo. 23, 1862; d.

CHILDREN OF JOHN AND LUCY R. TATUM.

Ashton R., b. 2 mo. 5, 1853.
Mary, b. 10 mo. 10, 1854.
John W., b. 1 mo. 28, 1857.
Amy, b. 12 mo. 21, 1858; d. in infancy.
Frances C., b. 9 mo. 18. 1861.
Elizabeth H., b. 4 mo. 18, 1868.

CHILDREN OF JOSEPH AND ANNA BRINGHURST.

John R., b. 1 mo. 8. 1845; d.   ; m. 2 mo. 17, 1870, Elizabeth Tatnall. Two children. His wife died 1 mo. 19, 1874.

Margaret R., b. 11 mo. 13, 1847; d.

Anna, b. 10 mo. 9. 1856; d.

CHILDREN OF CHARLES AND MARY WARNER.

Margaret R., b. 10 mo. 7. 1844; d.   ; m. 5 mo.   1868.
Linton Smith. Two children.

Alfred D., b. 9 mo. 10, 1847; d.   ; m. 5 mo.   1873. Emma B. Pusey. One child.

CHILDREN OF JOHN AND MARTHA RICHARDSON.

Mary A., b. 2 mo. 20. 1857; d.

John, b. 3 mo. 27. 1863; d.

Anna B., b. 1 mo. 12. 1865; d.

CHILDREN OF JOSEPH P. AND SARAH RICHARDSON.

Margaret, b. 8 mo. 15. 1857; d.

William, b. 5 mo. 1, 1859; d. 1859.

Elizabeth T., b. 1 mo. 30. 1862; d. young.

Sarah A., b. 11 mo. 2. 1863; d.

Martha, b. 11 mo. 27. 1865; d.

Edward A., b. 6 mo. 8. 1869; d.

Rodman, b. 5 mo. 30. 1871; d. young.

SEVENTH GENERATION.

CHILDREN OF BENJAMIN C. AND SARAH WILCOX.

CHILDREN OF DR. AND MARY MAXWELL.

CHILDREN OF J. SELLERS AND ANN S. BANCROFT.

Wilfred.
Alice,

CHILDREN OF J. SELLERS AND ELIZABETH BANCROFT.

Edward,
Henry,

CHILDREN OF SAMUEL AND MARY BANCROFT.

Elizabeth B.,
Joseph,

CHILDREN OF JOSHUA AND JANE PUSEY.

Elizabeth,
S. Richardson.

CHILDREN OF GILBERT AND LUCY CAMERON.

Mary,
Jessie,

CHILDREN OF HENRY B. AND SARAH RICHARDSON.

Anna S., b.

Agnes Y., b.

CHILDREN OF DR. SETH AND SARAH S. PANCOAST.

Ada B., b. 11 mo. 6, 1853; d.   ; m. 10 mo. 21, 1874, Emil
    Fink. Two children.

Sallie E., b. 12 mo. 9, 1856; d.

Laura P., b. 11 mo. 29, 1859; d.

CHILDREN OF DR. SETH AND SUSAN G. PANCOAST.

Mary Stroud, b. 3 mo. 15, 1870; d.

George, b. 7 mo. 1, 1871; d. 10 mo. 2, 1871.

Henry K., b. 2 mo. 26, 1875; d.

CHILDREN OF HENRY AND ANNA HALDERMAN.

Elizabeth, b. 9 mo. 28, 1858; d.

Carrie, b. 11 mo. 9, 1860; d.

CHILDREN OF EDWARD AND MARY E. STROUD.

Clara E., b. 4 mo. 1, 1857.

Mary E., b. 7 mo. 15, 1858.

Martha J., b. 9 mo. 23, 1861.

Franklin R., b. 10 mo. 15, 1863.

Henry R., b. 7 mo. 17, 1866.

Walter E., b. 5 mo. 23, 1870.

CHILDREN OF WM. J. AND CLARA E. STROUD.

Louis A., b. 1 mo. 28, 1863; d. 10 mo. 21, 1865.

Anna H., } Twins, b. 8 mo. 24, 1864.
Ella P., }

Alfred G., b. 9 mo. 15, 1866.
Samuel C., b. 5 mo. 26, 1870.
William M., b. 7 mo. 6, 1875.

CHILDREN OF ALFRED AND HANNAH J. GAWTHROP.

William J., b. 4 mo. 6, 1867.
Charles S., b. 11 mo. 21, 1868.
Bessie S., b. 8 mo. 4, 1870.
Sarah N., b. 10 mo. 6, 1874.

CHILDREN OF CLARKSON AND ELIZABETH S. TAYLOR.

Frank,
Charles, died young.
Henry M.,
William G., died young.
Edward M.,
Elizabeth,

CHILDREN OF EDWARD AND LYDIA S. MENDINHALL.

Sarah R.,
John M.,
Caroline H.,
Mary W., died young.

CHILDREN OF HENRY AND ELIZABETH W. MENDINHALL.

Jessie,
Eleanor W.,

CHILDREN OF GRANVILLE AND MARY S. WORRELL.

William G.,
Sarah W.,
Thomas,

8

CHILDREN OF GEO. W. AND ELIZ. T. SCARBOROUGH.

John Hedges, b. 5 mo. 22, 1862.
Maggie D., b. 10 mo. 11, 1864.
George Walter, b. 5 mo. 38, 1867.
James Wilton, b. 1 mo. 19, 1870.
William Sutton, b. 1 mo. 15, 1873.

CHILDREN OF JOHN C. AND MARY B. PIEL.

Mary Adeline, b. 2 mo. 28, 1867.
John Charles, b. 12 mo. 15, 1868.

CHILDREN OF CHARLES FRANKLIN AND FANNY STROU

William F., b. 11 mo. 1, 1868.
Laura H., b. 2 mo. 28, 1872.
Edgar M., b. 8 mo. 30, 1874.

CHILDREN OF JOHN H. AND EMMA STROUD.

James B., b. 8 mo. 25, 1868.

CHILDREN OF JAMES C. AND ADELINE E. WILSON.

Clarence, b. 5 mo. 29, 1871.
Raymond J., b. 7 mo. 13, 1873.

CHILDREN OF JONATHAN T. AND SALLY I. PURCEL.

Mary, b. 9 mo. 21, 1877.

CHILDREN OF HENRY AND MARY R. ALBERTSON.

William H., b. 3 mo. 2, 1873.
Amy, b. 11 mo. 29, 1874.
Elizabeth R., b. 9 mo. 18, 1876.

CHILDREN OF EDWARD AND RACHEL TATNALL.

Robert R.,
Samuel A..

CHILDREN OF ROBERT AND MARY R. BROWN.

Joseph T., died in infancy.
Henry.

CHILDREN OF JOHN R. AND ELIZ. BRINGHURST.

Joseph.
Frederick.

CHILDREN OF LINTON AND MARGARET R. SMITH.

Charles W.
Bertha.

CHILDREN OF ALFRED AND EMMA B. WARNER.

Charles,

EIGHTH GENERATION.

CHILDREN OF EMIL AND ADA B. FINK.

Carl, b. 8 mo. 4, 1875; d. 11 mo. 30, 1876.
Anna, b. 2 mo. 26, 1877.